CLOSE TO HOME

BY JOHN McPHERSON

Andrews and McMeel
A Universal Press Syndicate Company
Kansas City

ISBN: 0-8362-1750-0

Library of Congress Catalog Card Number: 93-74368

For Keith

"Tell us about the time you blocked the field goal and saved the big game against Penn State, Grandpa."

"Apparently I have done something to upset you."

"You kids drive me nuts! All day long you pester me about ice cream and now you aren't hungry!"

One of the 10 warning signs that the honeymoon is over.

"Leave the kitty alone, dear."

"The dog ate my headphones."

"Leaving handprints is for wimps!"

"Now what have I told you? Never bother Mommy when she's in the bathroom!"

"I'll be there in a second, dear. I'm tucking the kids in."

"I made these out of leftovers from Thanksgiving dinner. They're gravy Popsicles."

"Sorry about the mix-up, Mr. Bixford. We'll be moving you to a semi-private room shortly."

"Uhh ... Excuse me, ma'am but you've ... uh ... taken my cart by mistake. I believe that's yours there."

15

"Yeah, I know she shouldn't play with her food.
But that's pretty good!"

"Try jiggling the handle."

"You wouldn't believe the money we save by buying remnants."

"Not only is it good exercise for Bob, it's also great entertainment for the kids."

"Nah, it's still not quite right. Put in more worms."

"I can't believe you cleaned up your entire room
in five minutes."

	ONIONS	PEAS	CORN	BEANS	SPINACH
MIKE	HATES THEM	LIKES THEM	LIKES IT	HATES THEM	LIKES IT
TIM	LIKES THEM	HATES THEM	LOVES IT	HATES THEM	HATES IT
KATIE	LIKES THEM	HATES THEM	GAGS	GAGS	TOLERATES IT
LISA	Allergic	HATES THEM	Allerg.	Allerg.	HATES IT
WILLIE	THROWS THEM	TOLERATES THEM	THROWS IT	THROWS	THROWS

**"And over here we have Tyler's 'Blue Period.'
Notice the strong, sweeping strokes that
seem to leap right off the canvas."**

Budget wedding photos

"I don't know how we got by before we had the
automatic teller machine installed."

22

"My! What a good burp *that* was! Let's have one more now."

"So, is this your first baby?"

"Wow! That was neat! OK, now try it on high!"

"I'm concerned about his thumbsucking."

"And I better not find you kids shaking those presents to try and figure out what they are."

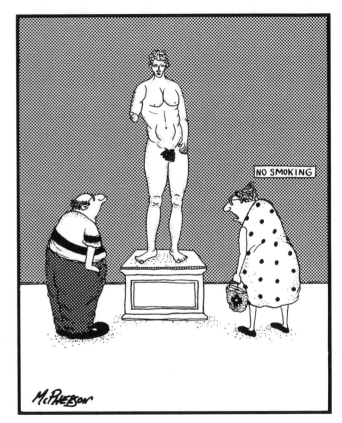

NO SMOKING

"I wish you'd renew your membership at the health club."

"Roger, we've been over this before. I need my closet space. Besides, there's more room for your clothes down here."

"I'll give you five bucks if you'll put eight miles on this thing before your father gets home."

"Whoops! Sorry I missed that rest area. Oh, well. The sign says there's another one in 76 miles."

"Well, thank you, Beth Ann! I'll put this up on the refrigerator right now!"

29

How to toddler-proof your home.

"Howard, I'm cold. Put on two more cats."

"Sorry, Mom. I thought I had enough momentum to clear the house."

"OK! Who's the wise guy who put the Mr. Yuk sticker on my turnip casserole?!"

"Wonderful news, George! Your cousin Freddie got a job selling vinyl siding!"

"Sorry, sir. We've still got a few bugs to work out."

"Now, here's the funny part, Dad."

"This is *not* what I had in mind when I asked you to take the baby for a stroll."

"Do me a favor and act like there's nothing wrong with it. My dad's pretty proud of the fact that he put it together all by himself."

"Well, my husband and I talked it over and agreed that it just isn't practical for us to own a sports car, so we decided it was best to sell it."

38

"So, tonight's the night you meet your future in-laws, eh? Whoops! Sorry about that."

"The batteries to the remote are getting weak."

"Here's part of an old cheeseburger, and I think
I can feel a couple more french fries."

"I don't like the looks of this storm."

"I can't believe you spent 150 bucks for those Rollerblades when I was able to make these for less than 30 bucks!"

The agony of living with a cold-footed spouse.

41

"How many times do I have to tell you kids to stop giving each other shocks?
You're scuffing up my rug!"

"For the last time, we are *not* buying an exercise bike!"

"Operator, get me the chocolate abuse hotline!"

"Sorry about this, Mark. My dad has a tendency
to be a little overprotective."

A cure for snoring

"This? This is Ninja Turtle soup."

"Are you gonna make me return the chemistry set?"

"You must have punched in the wrong four-digit number."

"And this little piggy faked left and ran up the middle for a 28-yard gain."

"The best part of it is I made this quilt entirely out of material
I found around the house."

48

Walt Nordman was not a morning person.

"We get 984 channels now,
thanks to this new cable."

Helen tries out her new
"Not-Tonight-Honey" nightgown.

How to make your wife hysterical

"Two or three months ago I was always exhausted because he needed constant attention. Now that he's able to entertain himself, life is *so* much easier."

"I'll take six hamburgers, four small fries, four Cokes, and a hundred napkins."

"I was just standing there in the yard when Art Nabro threw a snowball at me.
So I threw one back. Then he threw a bigger one back at me.
I threw an even *bigger* one back at him ..."

Just a typical morning for a one-bathroom couple.

"Can't you do something for this static cling?"

"You got any bright ideas how to get a peanut butter and jelly sandwich out of the VCR?"

Peggy's chances of getting a second date with Jack Mangiante took a turn for the worse when her dad started playing the theme to "Gilligan's Island" on his teeth.

The growing interest in health and fitness has had an effect on even the longest-standing traditions.

"Take the next right."

"Mom, he is *not* a date! Danny and I are just friends."

"Down boy!"

"Lucy, I think we need to have a talk about this little stenciling project of yours."

"I haven't gotten to that part yet!"

"Next time ask for paper."

The dream appliance for new parents.

"Here's the problem. The batteries to the garage door opener are in backwards."

"Vern and I have very different tastes when it comes to decorating, but we've been able to compromise pretty well."

"Here's another one of Rowena waving! That's the World Trade Center in the background, and if you look closely..."

63

"Oh, nothing. I just finished resealing the driveway and Ann is out getting some groceries. What's up with you?"

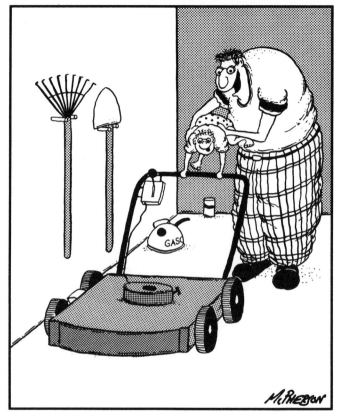

"And here's a little piece of equipment you're going to get to know *real* well, Danny. That's it, get used to the feel of the handle. Good!"

"Hey, you want to sleep through the night, don't you?"

"That's what we get for buying the
cheapest brand of fabric softener."

"Are you sure this is the honeymoon suite?"

"There! You felt it kick *that* time, didn't you?"

"Sorry, Steve. It looks like you're closest to the garter."

"The toy manufacturers finally got smart and came up with a puzzle that kids can't lose the pieces to."

"This is *not* what I had in mind when I said I wanted us to add a master bathroom!"

"Sorry about this. My dad wouldn't let me borrow the car."

Aerobics for couch potatoes

70

"I've got the thing wired up to a generator in the basement. We cut our electric bill in half last year."

"The seat that came with the bike was too darned uncomfortable."

"How 'bout those crazy jet streams?!"

"Norm's gotten a little bit lax lately when it comes to cutting firewood."

"You didn't happen to see the lid to the blender come through here, did you?"

A curfew was not something to be taken lightly in the Anderson household.

"Hey, Dad. I heard an interesting story. Did you know that Einstein failed math?! Really, it's true! Pretty amazing, huh, Dad?! Smart guy like Einstein doing crummy at math."

"How much longer are you going to be on this diet?"

"I do *not* want you feeding the dog scraps
at the dinner table!"

"We couldn't find any rice, so we're using mashed potatoes instead."

"I think we'll all be relieved when this rain lets up."

"That's exactly what he wants you to do, Al. Can't you see this is just a ploy to get attention? Don't give him the satisfaction of knowing that his behavior upsets you."

Every high school student's worst enemy: the essay question.

"I fell asleep in the tub."

"Whatever you do, don't tell Mom he's here."

"OK, now the left nostril. Good!"

"You'll get your $50 deposit back as long as you bring Darlene home by midnight."

81

"And here you can clearly see the baby's head and ... oh, look!
He's wiggling his toes there!"

82

"Stan, will you knock it off! He will walk
when he's ready to walk!"

"What are the chances I could get a $7,000
advance on my allowance?"

84

The '90s dad: able to spend time with his kids while still indulging in his favorite sport.

"Wow! First a drum and now cymbals! Thanks, Grandma and Grandpa!"

The Menlop brothers drop their dad some subtle hints that they want a bigger TV.

"All right now, give Mommy the Super Glue."

"The funny thing is, Dad, I was only going 10 miles an hour when it happened."

"Here's the problem! The workout tape has been on fast-forward the whole time!"

"That's a false eyelash."

"Exhale."

"I appreciate the fact that you're trying to be chivalrous, Kyle, but you were supposed to throw your coat over the puddle."

The older generation fights back.

"Oh look at you! Who says you need a new prom dress?!
My old dress fits you perfectly!"

"You guys didn't happen to see my science project come crawling through here, did you?"

"We were running out of room for the kids' drawings so we had to get another refrigerator."

Never let your parents chaperone a school dance.

"We know this is a bit unusual, Mrs. Glenmont. But since we've never hired a baby-sitter before, I'm sure you can understand that we're just taking some precautions."

"Are you serious? Your dad actually put a meter on the TV and if we want to watch the rest of 'Beverly Hills 90210' we need to put in $1.75?"

"Are you sure you checked out this place's references?"

"According to the on-board calorie computer, you burned the equivalent of three M&M's."

"Not only do we know you're not the real Easter Bunny, Dad,
you look like a complete bonehead!"

Wayne Pelnard was obsessed with winning the $10,000 prize on "America's Funniest Home Videos."

Thus far, Frank wasn't too impressed with the company's dental plan.

Marge had worked out a little signal to let her husband know when he was spending too much time in the shower.

Going to the same school as your younger brother can be an agonizing experience.

"Don found a way to wire the baby monitor into the stereo."

"What are you mad at me for? You're the one who bought me this cologne."

"Looks like that mower of yours starts a little hard."

Wendy was starting to sense that her dad wasn't overly impressed
with her new boyfriend.

"Well, I'd like to see the section in your health book that says pregnant women shouldn't cook!"

The downside of car pooling

Stella's father should have known better than to try to answer the phone when she was expecting calls from potential prom dates.

"You folks holler if that's too much air
for you back there."

"It's recycled aluminum siding."

"I see you had a little problem with the Weed Eater."

How to stop a blanket hog.

"Here it is! Glerf! It means 'Oprah's on'!"

"I forgot to bring my notebook to algebra today."

"For cryin' out loud! Would you just take a sick day for once in your life!"

Ranch houses have taken some of the thrill out of eloping.

Unfortunately for Dominique, neither the
Super-Stepper nor the accompanying
cassette tape was refundable.

"Lois, go over and help your father get the
child-proof cap off the aspirin."

111

"I've told you a hundred times! Always check the lawn
for foreign objects before you mow!"

How to embarrass your spouse.

"Hey, Mike, I think you forgot your lunch again."

"Yeah, I know your contractions are only two minutes apart. But if you can just hang in there until tomorrow, I'll win the baby pool at work."

"I am *not* doting on you! I just want you to look good for your big meeting, hon. Now let me fix this collar."

"You must have dozed off for quite a while."

Students weren't too fond of the new enlarged report cards.

"Oh, Delores, you lucky girl! You caught the bouquet!"

"Well, thank you, Wayne and Elwin. An Assault of the Psycho Slime Monsters Nintendo cartridge. How thoughtful of you."

"According to our data, a small hole in the ozone layer has opened up directly above your house."

"Boy! That was some pothole!"

"Hey, kids! We've got a lot more string here than I thought! Look at that baby! I'm gonna just keep letting it out!"

"I'm afraid that wisdom tooth is impacted."

"I got sick and tired of putting her in and out of the car seat, so I finally just said the heck with it."

"I realize this may affect your playing, but those darned squeaky sneakers drive me nuts."

"Dee Dee Vershay's dog is having a hernia operation. Everybody's signing this get-well card and kicking in $10."

"Yeah, we used to put out three cans of garbage a week. Since we started composting, we're down to one can."

Louis Wrzynski's lifelong fascination with dominoes culminated in this one fateful moment.

123

"The dog ate the remote again."

How to get a teen-ager to mow the lawn.

"All I can say is, next time I'll know better when somebody offers me a free car phone for just opening a new checking account."

"Yeah, when we were shopping for garbage disposals, we figured we might as well spend the extra hundred bucks and get the combination disposal/mulcher."

125

"Bummer."

"His high school reunion is tomorrow."

The modern-day widow's watch

"Psst! Make sure you get her home by midnight!"